D0623921

digging in the dirt

A Kid's Guide to How Trees Grow

Patricia Ayers

The Rosen Publishing Group's
PowerKids Press™
New York

Published in 2000 by The Rosen Publishing Group, Inc.
29 East 21st Street, New York, NY 10010

First Edition

Book Design: Maria Melendez

Photo Credits: Cover and title page, pp. 1, 6, 10, 11, 15, 16, 19, 20, 21 © Tony Stone Images; pp. 1, 3, 4, 11 © FPG International; p.4, 6, 8, 9, 12, 14 © Super Stock; p. 7, 8, 9, 11 © International Stock

Ayers, Patricia.
        A kid's guide to how trees grow / by Patricia Ayers.
        p.   cm. — (The Digging in the dirt series)
    Includes index.
    Summary: Explains the basics of how different kinds of trees grow.
    ISBN: 0-8239-5463-3 (lib. bdg.)
    1. Trees Juvenile literature.   2. Trees, Care of Juvenile literature.
    [1. Trees.] I. Title. II. Series: Ayers, Patricia. Digging in the dirt series.

     SB435.A97 1999
     635.9'77—dc21   99-23319
                                                      CIP
                                                       AC

Manufactured in the United States of America.

Contents

Bristlecone pines

Redwood trees

Redwood tree trunk

Pinecones

Old and Wise

Trees are the oldest living things on earth. Some bristlecone pines are 4,000 years old. The sequoias, or redwood trees, in California are several thousand years old. Some trees are as big as buildings! They can be almost 300 feet tall and 30 feet wide. It's amazing to think that they started as a tiny seed from inside a cone.

Unlike people and animals, trees keep growing for as long as they live. Their trunks add a layer to their width each year. When a tree is cut down you can count the layers, or rings, to tell its age.

◀ *Some trees can live for thousands of years.*

Quiet at Work

You'd never guess all the work that goes on under the bark of a quiet-looking tree. The sugar maple tree, for example, is reading the light and temperature around itself all the time. When there is not enough light or warmth, the tree becomes **dormant**, or goes to sleep. When it is warm again, the tree wakes up and starts making sugary **sap** again.

Special cells in the tree trunk carry minerals and water up the tree, from the roots to the leaves. Other cells carry sap from the leaves back down to the roots. A large sugar maple tree can make 40 gallons of sap, which will make one gallon of delicious maple syrup!

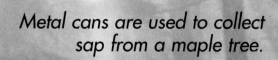

Metal cans are used to collect sap from a maple tree. ▷

Kinds of Trees

There are about 20,000 different kinds of trees in the world. All trees are **perennials**, meaning they live longer than one season. They all have a single main stem or trunk. Branches grow from this main stem and leaves grow from the branches. The leaves that grow on trees come in many different sizes and shapes. Did you know that each **species** of tree has a different shaped leaf?

There are two main types of trees, evergreen and **deciduous**. Evergreen trees always look green and do not lose their leaves in the fall. The leaves of deciduous trees change color in the fall. Then the leaves drop to the ground so the tree is bare.

◀ *Can you tell which trees are deciduous and which are evergreen?*

The Evergreen Family

The world's oldest trees belong to the evergreen family. Evergreens include pine, fir, and spruce trees. Trees in the evergreen family are called **conifers**, which means they have needle-shaped leaves and grow cones. Did you know that tiny seeds lie at the bottom of the cones?

These trees are called evergreens because their needle-shaped leaves seem to stay green forever. Each needle lives anywhere from 2 to 10 years. Then these needles drop off the tree and turn brown. Their new, green replacements keep the tree looking green. Evergreen trees live mainly in cold **climates**, and their needles have a hard coating that helps them live through icy winters.

The leaves of evergreen trees have learned to survive in a cold environment. ▷

Fir and pine forest

Fir trees in snow

Spruce needles

Autumn leaves and pine needles

Red and Yellow Leaves

Have you ever wondered why the leaves of some trees change color in the fall? A green chemical called **chlorophyll** makes leaves green. Trees use chlorophyll and energy from sunlight to turn water and nutrients into sugar that the tree can eat. This process is called **photosynthesis**. When days get colder and darker in the fall, chlorophyll breaks down. The leaves change color because they are no longer filled with this green chlorophyll. Without this chlorophyll, the leaves can't make food anymore, and they die. That's why they fall off the tree.

◀ *Leaves change color because they lose a green substance called chlorophyll.*

Celebrating Trees

Trees even have a special day in late April named for them. It's called Arbor Day. To celebrate the importance of trees, people get together to plant them. Sarah's school principal, Mrs. Dino, organized each class to plant trees around the new playground on Arbor Day. Like all plants, trees grow well only in the right climates and soils.

The classes were asked to look around and report what kinds of trees grew near their school. Then they had to find out if their soil had the right nutrients. A gardener came to their school and tested the soil. She told the students to dig up the soil, and mix it with some **fertilizer** to make a loose, airy bed.

Arbor Day is a great day to plant your own tree. ▷

The Root of It All

The class needed to make a good soil bed for the tree so its roots would be able to grow. Tree roots help hold the soil together. The roots, which are covered with tiny hairs, spread out underground. They weave a kind of net that holds dirt in place. This way, trees help prevent **erosion**, or dirt being blown or carried away by water. If you see a tree that has been uprooted, take a close look at the huge roots. They can be three times as long as the tree's branches, and many feet deep.

◀ *Roots take in nutrients and water from the soil.*

17

Self-Seeders

Most trees are self-seeders, which means that they grow wherever their seeds fall onto the ground. Some seeds, like acorns, drop off the tree and fall to the ground where they can be planted. Birds and other animals may carry other seeds farther away from the tree. The wind carries the most seeds. The seeds settle into the ground, and if conditions are right, they will **germinate**, or sprout, and grow into **seedlings**. In the woods, where there are lots of trees, the ground is covered with tiny seedlings competing for sun, food, and space. The seedlings that get the food and light they need will grow into healthy trees.

18

Inside of these cones are many seeds. Some of them will settle into the ▷ earth and grow into trees.

Digging In

The students chose to plant crabapple trees for their beautiful spring flowers, peach trees for their fruit, and pine trees for their evergreen beauty. Mrs. Dino bought these tree seedlings and young trees from a nursery. Sarah and the other students dug holes as deep as the small trees' roots had been growing, but much wider, to encourage the roots to spread. They planted each tree and watered it until there was a puddle in the dirt around the trunk. Then they patted down the dirt to make each tree stand firm. The students checked every day to make sure the tree bed was not too dry. Then they watched their trees grow up, branch out, and grow leaves!

◀ *You can grow your own pine tree from a young sapling.*

21

What Trees Do

Trees help us live. Their leaves take in **carbon dioxide** from the air and release oxygen. People need oxygen to stay alive and breathe out carbon dioxide as waste.

Special cells in the tree trunk pull water up from the roots to the tips of the trees. By opening and closing tiny holes, leaves send water out into the air. This is called **transpiration**. A big oak may put 28,000 gallons of water into the air each year. This water will make its way into clouds, and it will later fall to the earth as rain. This rainwater will then feed more trees!

Glossary

carbon dioxide (KAR-bin dy-OK-syd) A gas that plants take in from the air and use to make food.

chlorophyll (KLOR-a-fil) A green substance in leaves and plants.

climates (KLY-mits) Weather conditions in certain places; the temperature, humidity, winds, and rainfall.

conifers (KAH-nih-furz) Types of trees that have needle-like leaves and grow cones.

deciduous (duh-SIHD-yoo-us) Shedding leaves annually.

dormant (DOR-ment) Asleep, temporarily inactive.

erosion (eh-RO-shen) The process of wearing away the surface of the earth.

fertilizer (FUR-til-y-zer) A substance put in soil to help crops grow.

germinate (JER-ma-nayt) To begin growing or sprouting.

perennials (per-EN-ee-ulz) Plants that live for more than two years.

photosynthesis (foh-toh-SIN-thuh-sis) The process where carbon dioxide and water, in the presence of light and chlorophyll, are changed into sugar, the energy-rich food used by plants.

sap (SAP) The liquid that circulates through a plant, carrying food and water.

seedlings (SEED-lingz) Young plants grown from a seed.

species (SPEE-sheez) A group of living things that have some of the same features.

transpiration (tran-spuh-RAY-shun) Giving off moisture through tiny pores in leaves.

Index

Web Sites:
You can learn more about trees at these Web sites:
http://www.evergreenshowplace.com/deciduus.html
http://www3.garden.com/cgi
http://www.esf.edu/pubprog/brochure/leaves/leaves.htm